W9-AHK-223

LIFE CYCLES

The Kangaroo

Diana Noonan

CHELSEA CLUBHOUSE

An Imprint of Chelsea House Publishers
A Haights Cross Communications Company

Philadelphia

This edition first published in 2003 in the United States of America by Chelsea Clubhouse, a division of Chelsea House Publishers and a subsidiary of Haights Cross Communications.

Chelsea Clubhouse
1974 Sproul Road, Suite 400
Broomall, PA 19008-0914

The Chelsea House world wide web address is www.chelseahouse.com

Library of Congress Cataloging-in-Publication Data

Noonan, Diana.
    The kangaroo / by Diana Noonan.
    p. cm. — (Life cycles)
    Summary: An introduction to the physical characteristics, behavior, and birth and development of kangaroos, marsupials that live in Australia.
    ISBN 0-7910-6968-0
    1. Kangaroos—Life cycles—Juvenile literature. [1. Kangaroos.] I. Title. II. Series
    QL737.M35 N66 2003
    599.2'22—dc21

                                                                            2002000036

First published in 1999 by
MACMILLAN EDUCATION AUSTRALIA PTY LTD
627 Chapel Street, South Yarra, Australia, 3141

Copyright © Diana Noonan 1999
Copyright in photographs © individual photographers as credited

Edited by Anne McKenna
Text design by Polar Design
Cover design by Linda Forss

Printed in China

Acknowledgements
Cover: Eastern gray kangaroos: female and joey. (© Jean-Paul Ferrero/Auscape)

A.N.T. Photo Library, pp. 4, 8, 26, 28 © Dave Watts, 5, 14 © Otto Rogge, 6, 12 & 30, 24, 25 & 30 © Tony Howard, 10 © Michael Cermak, 11 © Fredy Mercay, 13 © Jack Cameron, 15 © G. & R. Wilson; Auscape, pp. 7 & 30, 9, 16, 17 & 30, 18, 19 & 30, 23, 29 © Jean-Paul Ferrero, 21 © Mark Spencer, 27 © John Cancalosi; Australian Picture Library, pp. 20 © John Carnemolla, 22 © Gary Bell.

While every care has been taken to trace and acknowledge copyright, the publisher tenders their apologies for any accidental infringement where copyright has proved untraceable.

Contents

Life Cycles

All animals change as they live and grow. They begin life as tiny creatures. They become adults that will produce their own young. The kangaroo has its own special life cycle.

Kangaroos Are Mammals

Kangaroos belong to a group of animals called mammals. Mammals are covered with hair or fur. Female mammals give birth to live young. They feed their young milk from their own bodies.

Mammals are warm-blooded animals. Their body temperature stays the same. It does not matter how warm or cold the air or water is around them.

Marsupials

The kangaroo is an unusual mammal. It belongs to the marsupial family. Marsupials are very tiny when they are born. They grow in a **pouch** on their mother's skin. They live there until they are old enough to help look after themselves.

This young kangaroo lives in its mother's pouch.

Living in Mobs

Kangaroos live in warm, dry areas of Australia. They form family groups called mobs. Each mob has a few adult males, several females, and their young. One adult male is the leader. Younger kangaroos and some adults may join other mobs. Mobs are bigger when there is a lot of food available.

Nocturnal Feeders

Kangaroos eat grasses and other small plants. Most kangaroos are nocturnal feeders. They eat at night or in the early morning when the weather is cool.

Kangaroos rest in shady places during the day. Sometimes they dig **hollows** in the ground where they can stay cool.

A kangaroo rests in the shade.

Drinking

Kangaroos drink from creeks and pools. They also dig holes to find water. Kangaroos receive some water from the plants they eat. Some kangaroos can go for many weeks without drinking.

Courting and Mating

A female kangaroo is ready to **mate** when she is between 18 months and 3 years old. Male kangaroos are ready to mate when they are about 3 years old.

A male fights for the chance to mate with a female. He kicks and boxes other males. He snorts to warn them to keep away. The male who wins then **courts** the female for one or two hours before he mates with her.

These male kangaroos are fighting over a mate.

Birth

The female is ready to give birth about five weeks after mating. She uses her tongue to lick the inside of her pouch clean.

A female cleans her pouch.

A newborn kangaroo is very small.

A newborn kangaroo is about 1 inch
(2.5 centimeters) long. It is blind and deaf.
It has no fur. The young kangaroo has soft
cartilage instead of bones.

Into the Pouch

The tiny kangaroo pulls itself up its mother's fur with its strong front legs. It uses its sense of smell to find its way into its mother's pouch.

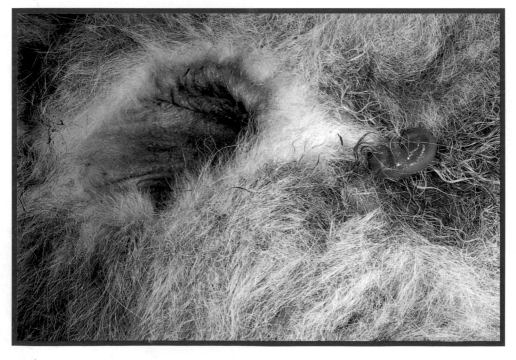

This newborn kangaroo climbs toward its mother's pouch.

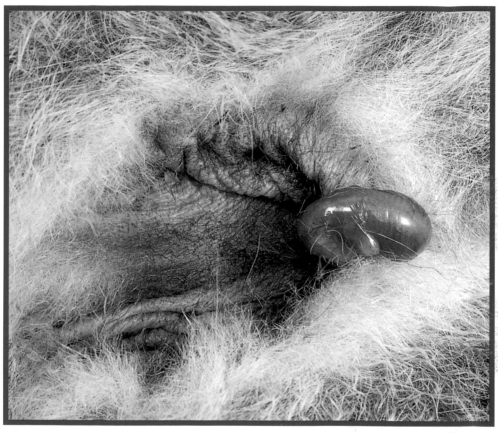

The newborn kangaroo climbs into the pouch.

The journey to the pouch takes about three minutes. The mother kangaroo does not help her **newborn**.

The Newborn

Female kangaroos have four **teats** in their pouch. The newborn kangaroo sucks on one of the teats.

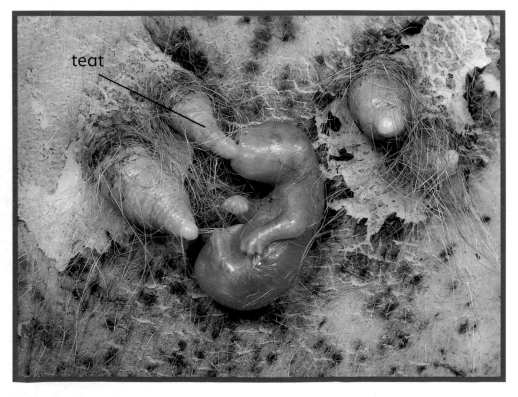

This newborn is 3 to 4 days old.

teat

This kangaroo is 3 weeks old.

The teat swells in the newborn's mouth and holds it safely in place. The newborn can now feed on its mother's milk.

The mother kangaroo uses her strong muscles to hold her pouch closed. The muscles seal the pouch to keep out water when she goes swimming.

The Joey

A newborn kangaroo grows very quickly.
When it is about 4 months old it is called a
joey. It is about the size of a cat and has
fur on its body.

Leaving the Pouch

The joey can leave its mother's pouch when it is about 5 months old. It stays outside the pouch for only short periods. The joey learns to hop on its strong back legs.

This joey is 5 months old.

The Young-at-Heel

The joey leaves its mother's pouch for the last time. It is just over 7 months old. Now it is called a **young-at-heel**.

A young-at-heel still drinks milk from its mother's teat. It stays close to its mother until it is about 20 months old.

A young-at-heel drinks milk from its mother.

Breeding Cycle

The female kangaroo raises many young at once. The young-at-heel leaves her pouch. Then she gives birth to a newborn. She quickly mates again.

A female takes care of her young kangaroo.

The female kangaroo can sense if a drought or other difficult times may be coming. Her body sends a message to the unborn kangaroo in her **womb**. The message tells the unborn kangaroo not to grow until conditions improve.

Kangaroos can sense when a drought is coming.

young-at-heel

joey

A female usually has a new kangaroo
growing in her womb, a newborn or a joey
in her pouch, and a young-at-heel close by.

A female kangaroo makes a different type of milk for each of the young she is feeding. The newborn or joey drinks from one teat. The young-at-heel drinks a different kind of milk from another teat.

Life Span

Kangaroos may live as long as 15 to 20 years. Female kangaroos stay with their young. They feed and protect their young until they can look after themselves. A young kangaroo has a very good chance of growing into an adult and having young of its own.

The Life Cycle of a Kangaroo

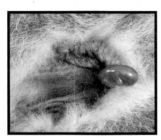

newborn climbs
into pouch

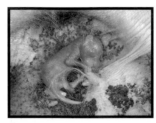

newborn latches
onto teat

adult kangaroo

joey lives in pouch

young-at-heel stays
close to mother

Glossary

cartilage　　strong tissue that may develop into bone as an animal grows

court　　to try to attract a mate

hollow　　a shallow hole

joey　　a young kangaroo that is between 4 and 7 months old; a joey lives in its mother's pouch.

mate　　to join with a breeding partner to produce young

newborn　　a baby kangaroo that is less than 4 months old

pouch　　a pocket of skin on a marsupial's body used for carrying its young

teat　　a part of a mother's body from which young drink milk

womb　　the place inside the female's body where a kangaroo grows before it is born

young-at-heel　　a young kangaroo that feeds from its mother but does not live in her pouch

Index